The Wit and Wisdom of Dolly Parton

FRANK JOHNSON

ISBN: 1503067815
ISBN-13: 978-1503067813

CONTENTS

INTRODUCTION

Dolly Parton is without doubt the most famous female country music legend around the world. While much of the genre never makes it out of America, Dolly has thrilled the world with songs such as 9 to 5, and has become a household name the world over.

Dolly is also known for her good looks and bubbly personality, which has added to her charm and perhaps contributed to her extensive fan base. She is also known for her extensive work as an actress and author.

Though exceptionally successful within her work, as her fans know there is much more to Dolly Parton that this. Well known as a philanthropist, her caring personality shines through everything she does and she is an outspoken and bold character.

This book brings together some of Dolly's most notable quotes on a large variety of topics.

ABOUT HER WORK

"I'm not going to limit myself just because people won't accept the fact that I can do something else."

*

"I write for myself things that I've gone through."

*

"I'm a workin' girl."

*

"I will not play just an evil part. In fact, I got offered $7 million several years ago to play the part that Faye Dunaway played in 'Supergirl.' I was kind of insulted. I was impressed with the money, but I said, 'Why are you asking me to play an evil witch? Do I come across as an evil witch to you?'"

*

"I am confident that partnering my Dollywood Company with a great company like Gaylord will create something truly special."

*

"I think every entertainer's had nights when things go wrong. I mean you can't remember everything all the time, and especially if you're having hard times personally, things going on that you - you know, and then people make it worse. And that makes you feel worse."

*

"I can be accused of trying to be commercial sometimes."

*

"I've enjoyed all the parts of my career."

*

"I'm working on my life story. I'm not decided if it's going to be a musical or a movie with music in it."

*

"Of course, 'I Will Always Love You' is the biggest song so far in my career. I'm famous for several, but that one has been recorded by more people and made me more money, I think, than all of them. But that song did come from a true and deep place in my heart."

*

"I can write a song in about an hour if it's a simple country song."

*

"I will never retire unless I have to."

*

"I've copyrighted 3,000 songs."

*

"I'm gonna be making records anyway, even if I had to sell 'em out of the trunk of my car. I'm that kind of musician and singer."

*

"I ain't never far away from a pencil and paper or a tape recorder."

*

"For some reason, I have better luck when I work with women. I guess I have a good sense of sisterhood."

*

"Songwriting is my way of channeling my feelings and my thoughts. Not just mine, but the things I see, the people I care about. My head would explode if I didn't get some of that stuff out."

*

"Writing's just as natural to me as getting up and cooking breakfast."

*

"I modelled my looks on the town tramp."

*

"A lot of my heartbreak songs are inspired by things my sisters are going through, or friends."

*

"Dollywood is a family park, and all families are welcome. We do have a policy about profanity or controversial messages on clothing or signs. It is to protect the individual wearing or carrying them, as well as to keep down fights or problems by those opposed to it at the park."

*

"My first job was singing on the Cas Walker radio show in Knoxville, Tennessee. I was about 10 years old, and I thought it was big time."

*

"I listen to my old records and I think, 'How did I ever get on the radio?'"

*

"My nails are my rhythm section when I'm writing a song all alone. Some day, I may cut an album, just me and my nails."

*

"I always think of myself as a working girl."

*

"I wanted to write a book that talked about the emotions of children, which is the rainbow. We all have moods. We talk about being blue when we're sad, and being yellow when we're cowards, and when we're mad, we're red."

*

"I'm a singer, a writer and an actress - when I find something that I feel good enough about doing."

*

"I've tried different things through the years to get some play on mainstream. I'll try to tailor-make it."

*

"A lot of people don't realise I came out of the

Smoky Mountains with a load of songs."

*

"Everywhere I go, the kids call me 'the book lady.' The older I get, the more appreciative I seem to be of the 'book lady' title. It makes me feel more like a legitimate person, not just a singer or an entertainer. But it makes me feel like I've done something good with my life and with my success."

*

"I know who I am, I know what I can and can't do. I know what I will and won't do. I know what I'm capable of and I don't agree to do things that I don't think I can pull off."

*

"My songs are like my children - I expect them to support me when I'm old."

*

"'9 to 5 the Musical' is perfect for anyone that's ever wanted to string up their boss, which is almost all of us."

*

"A lot of people have said I'd have probably done better in my career if I hadn't looked so cheap and gaudy. But I dress to be comfortable for me, and you shouldn't be blamed because you want to look pretty."

*

"I have suffered most of the things I write about - or my friends have."

*

"I'm pretty sure in my older years, I'll be doing old-time flavored folk-mountain music."

ABOUT MUSIC

"I always loved that old song 'Banks of the Ohio' - it was always such a man's song, so I've always wanted to record it."

*

"I love story songs because I've always loved books."

*

"Actually, I hear a lot of rock music. My husband is a big rock fan."

*

"If you talk bad about country music, it's like saying bad things about my momma. Them's fightin' words."

*

"I don't have time to stand around and listen to an 11-minute song."

*

"I was probably 7 years old when I started playing the guitar and writing some serious songs."

*

"I know it's corny - but I love 'Jingle Bells!'"

*

"Most country songs, certainly all the stuff I've

written, are stories driven by characters."

*

"I think country music is popular - has been popular and will always be popular because I think a lot of real people singing about a lot of real stuff about real people. And it's simple enough for people to understand it. And we kind of roll with the punches."

*

"I'm always amazed by the people who work on stage who sing night after night, day after day, week in week out."

ABOUT OTHER PEOPLE

"I say, 'Yeah, Taylor Swift.' I think she is a smart, beautiful girl. I think she's making all the right moves. She's got a good head on her shoulders. She's surrounded with wonderful people. Her songs are great. She keeps herself anchored. She knows who she is, and she's living and standing by that."

*

"Kitty Wells was the first and only Queen of Country Music, no matter what they call the rest of us. She was a great inspiration to me as well as every other female singer in the country music business. In addition to being a wonderful asset to country music, she was a wonderful woman."

*

"George Jones was my all-time favorite singer and one of my favorite people in the world."

*

"I'd love to do a duet, always wanted to work with Madonna, but she never asked."

*

"I used to sing songs and write with my uncle, Bill Owens."

*

"I'll be like Bob Hope, touring when I'm 100."

*

"I don't have anything to say about other people's art and their work."

*

"No one could have been nicer, classier nor better looking than Dick Clark. I've had a crush on him since I was a teenager."

*

"Mine is only one of the millions of hearts broken over the death of Whitney Houston, I will always be grateful and in awe of the wonderful performance she did on my song, and I can truly say from the bottom of my heart, 'Whitney, I will always love you. You will be missed.'"

GENERAL THOUGHTS & OPINIONS

"I think so many people live their whole life in fear and doubt and shame."

*

"I think 9/11 affected everybody in one way or another."

*

"There's nothing like white trash at the White House."

*

"When you're 40, you can't ride the fence anymore. You gotta make definite decisions about your life."

*

"There are certainly a lot of things that still need to change when it comes to women in the workforce."

*

"I do believe that any successful business starts from the top and works its way down."

*

"I think your values are always influenced by your family and your community."

*

"You don't need to buy expensive cosmetics; almost anything will do if you know how to apply it."

*

"People like bluegrass. It's had a following amongst a lot of hip and young people. A lot of college kids like bluegrass."

GOD & RELIGION

"I always ask God to work through me and let me be a light of some kind and help in this world, so I always pray for that, and I always want to do good."

*

"You don't see too many atheists on the deathbed. They all start cramming then."

*

"God and I have a great relationship, but we both see other people."

*

"Being brought up very religious, I have a fear of
people that look to idol gods."

*

"Every day I pray about all I do."

*

"I really learned to sing in church, I think, really
with emotion."

*

"I used to always sit in church looking out the
windows at the boys, wondering if I could make an
excuse to go out and, you know, go to the bathroom
because all the outdoor toilets. But anyhow, I was
only going out to see the boys."

*

"I thank God for my failures. Maybe not at the time but after some reflection. I never feel like a failure just because something I tried has failed."

*

"God tells us not to judge one another, no matter what anyone's sexual preferences are or if they're black, brown or purple."

*

"God has his plans and his reasons. Sometimes we are supposed to go through things so that we learn lessons."

HERSELF & HER FAMILY

"I've done everything every fat person ever has. I've tried every diet."

*

"When I was a little girl, I always dreamed of being a star. I didn't really know what all that meant. I didn't know."

*

"I have little bones."

*

"I was born with a happy heart, and I try to keep a good attitude. It's not true that I'm happy all the time because nobody is, and we all go through our things."

*

"I'm not intimidated by how people perceive me."

*

"Until I was a teenager, I used red pokeberries for lipstick and a burnt matchstick for eyeliner. I used honeysuckle for perfume."

*

"No matter what, I always make it home for Christmas. I love to go to my Tennessee Mountain Home and invite all of my nieces and nephews and their spouses and kids and do what we all like to do - eat, laugh, trade presents and just enjoy each other... and sometimes I even dress up like Santa Claus!"

*

"My mama never wore a pair of pants when I was growing up, and now that's all she wears. It was so funny for me when I first started seeing Mama wear pants. It was like it wasn't Mama. Now I've bought her many a pantsuit because she just lives in them."

*

"Nobody can ever make enough money for as many poor relatives as I've got. Somebody's got a sick kid, or somebody needs an operation, somebody ain't got this, somebody ain't got that. Or to give the kids all a car when they graduate."

*

"I love Velveeta cheese."

*

"I still close my eyes and go home - I can always draw from that."

*

"I'm not a politician. And I don't want to be."

*

"I had nothing growing up, but I always wanted to be 'sexy,' even before I knew what the word was."

*

"I don't think I'm supposed to boss other people around just because I'm a so-called celebrity or star. I hate that when people act that way. No one deserves it. I've seen it happen. I don't call those people out - they know who they are. Some enjoy that reputation."

*

"I love traveling all over the world; but it's true: there's nothing like home."

*

"I don't have maids or servants, and my husband and I love waking up early and going to the 24-hour supermarket when there is nobody else there."

*

"I do have a few little tattoos, but they were mostly done to cover scars because I'm so fair."

*

"I have a tendency to be awfully big-hearted and it's very hard for me to say no, even when I need to."

*

"You know, I look like a woman but I think like a man. And in this world of business, that has helped me a lot. Because by the time they think that I don't know what's goin' on, I then got the money, and gone."

*

"I'll bring my grits when I travel, because I get so hungry on the road."

*

"I usually get up at 3 A.M. I don't require a lot of sleep, and if I get tired, I'll take a powernap during the day."

*

"I'm no natural beauty. If I'm gonna have any looks at all, I'm gonna have to create them."

*

"I've used my femininity and my sexuality as a weapon and a tool... but that's just natural."

*

"People get a kick out of my stupidity."

*

"People make jokes about my bosoms, why don't they look underneath the breasts at the heart? It's obvious I've got big ones and if people want to assume they're not mine, then let them."

*

"I'm just a friendly person; that runs in my family."

*

"My favorite movies of all times is 'Doctor Zhivago,' and I love 'Gone With the Wind.' I'd love to play some Southern belle or something where I owned a plantation."

*

"I was very honored to get to be part of 'American Idol.'"

*

"After momma gave birth to 12 of us kids, we put her up on a pedestal. It was mostly to keep Daddy away from her."

*

"If I see something sagging, bagging or dragging I'll get it nipped, tucked or sucked."

*

"I'm a showgirl, as you can tell. I'm ever ready."

*

"When I got somethin' to say, I'll say it."

*

"I just don't have time to get old!"

*

"When I'm inspired, I get excited because I can't wait to see what I'll come up with next."

*

"I didn't know any gay people in my childhood."

*

"I can't tell anybody else how to run their life or their business, but I really believe I've got a good bead on myself."

*

"I am a tender-hearted person, and I feel everything to the ninth degree."

*

"I love Indian, Italian and Mexican food. And if it's a romantic type of thing, I like a good French restaurant."

*

"I love to flirt, and I've never met a man I didn't like."

*

"I just kind of wake up with a new idea and new dreams every day, and I follow that dream, as they say."

*

"Being a star just means that you just find your own special place, and that you shine where you are. To me, that's what being a star means."

*

"I'm old enough and cranky enough now that if someone tried to tell me what to do, I'd tell them where to put it."

*

"I have tennis shoes with little rhinestones that I slip on if I exercise. But I always wear heels, even around the house. I'm such a short little thing, I can't reach my kitchen cabinets."

*

"I think people take me as seriously as I want them to. They take me as seriously as I take myself - let's put it that way."

*

"I come from a family of 12, so I kind of got a little lost as a child."

*

"I'm not happy all the time, and I wouldn't want to be because that would make me a shallow person. But I do try to find the good in everybody."

*

"I walk tall; I got a tall attitude."

*

"My husband says I look like a Q-tip."

*

"My husband and I had to raise five of my younger brothers and sisters. They lived with us. We sent them to school."

*

"I wear make-up, and it gets a little bit thicker every year."

*

"My husband calls me 'catfish.' He says I'm all mouth and no brains."

*

"I try to see the good in everybody, and I don't care who people are as long as they're themselves, whatever that is."

*

"I think there is a little magic in the fact that I'm so totally real but look so artificial at the same time."

*

"I think I've got my business notions and my sense for that sort of thing from my dad. My dad never had a chance to go to school. He couldn't read and write. But he was so smart. He was just one of those people that could just make the most of anything and everything that he had to work with."

*

"I'll never graduate from collagen."

*

"If I can get my dress on, my weight is under control."

*

"I want to go and go, and then drop dead in the middle of something I'm loving to do. And if that doesn't happen, if I wind up sitting in a wheelchair, at least I'll have my high heels on."

*

"I was approached about having my own network many, many years ago. There were some people who wanted to start up a network, and I didn't want to get that involved in the business aspect of it."

*

"I met my husband before I became a star, and he doesn't care about any of it."

*

"Children have always responded to me because I have that cartoon-character look."

*

"Every seven years, I sit down and make a whole new plan."

*

"I can't keep somebody from being a star, and I can't make somebody a star, and nobody can."

*

"I've always been fascinated by everything with wings."

*

"I have had some cosmetic surgery, especially after I lost weight and stuff, and I've had my breasts lifted - but not injected. That would scare me to death, anyway."

*

"I've never had a divorce, but I've seen so many of my friends, my sister, my family go through that stuff, so I try to write for the people that can't write about it. I take on their sorrow, so I'm able to kind of express it, or their joy."

*

"I don't kiss nobody's butt."

*

"A gypsy told me I was going to do great things. I was going to make all kinds of money."

*

"I hated school. Even to this day, when I see a school bus it's just depressing to me. The poor little kids."

*

"I can't do nothing just a little."

*

"When I'm home, I spend Sunday with my husband. If we're not cooking, we travel around in our camper, stop at fast-food restaurants, and picnic. We love that stuff that will harden your arteries in a hurry."

*

"I've never been a feminist."

*

"I think that I know the value of a dollar."

*

"I always thought that if I made it big or got successful at what I had started out to do, that I wanted to come back to my part of the country and do something great, something that would bring a lot of jobs into this area."

*

"I am not gay, but if I were, I would be the first one running out of the closet."

*

"My life has been very full."

*

"I don't make people bend over backwards, and I don't like that in people. I am definitely no diva."

*

"I grew up around lots of men - my father, my brothers, my uncles - so I wasn't intimidated by them."

*

"Depression runs in my family on both sides, and I have to be wary."

*

"My weaknesses have always been food and men - in that order."

*

"I'm an energy vampire. I just suck off everybody's energy. But I give it back."

*

"I know that I always wanted things. I was always proud of my people, proud of my home, but I always wanted more. I think most people do."

*

"I wouldn't wanna go out not looking like the Dolly

people have come to know, because I've come to
know her that way, too."

*

"I love being busy."

*

"I always wanted to be loved."

*

"I'm just a simple country girl."

*

"When I wake up, I expect things to be good. If
they're not, then I try to set about trying to make
them as good as I can 'cause I know I'm gonna have
to live that day anyway. So why not try to make the
most of it if you can? Some days, they pan out a
little better than others, but you still gotta always
just try."

*

"Above everything else I've done, I've always said I've had more guts than I've got talent."

*

"I often joke that 100 years from now I hope people are saying, 'Dang, she looks good for her age!'"

*

"I have a big gay and lesbian following and they've been very loyal and kind to me."

*

"Oh, I can spot a phoney a mile away."

*

"My grandpa was a preacher."

*

"I'm almost like three people. There's me the, Dolly, the person. There's me, the star. And then there's me, the manager."

*

"I've always kinda been a little outcast myself, a little oddball, doin' my thing, my own way. And it's been hard for me to, to be accepted, certainly in the early years of my life."

*

"Thanks to Botox and fillers, as well as the work that I've already had, my face pretty much maintains itself."

*

"I wear wigs all the time on shows, and every day when I'm in public, at Dollywood. People say, 'How many wigs do you have?' And I say, 'Well, at least 365 because I wear at least one a day.'"

*

"A lot of people think I'm a comedian."

*

"I look at myself like a show dog. I've got to keep her clipped and trimmed and in good shape."

*

"It's a good thing I was born a girl, otherwise I'd be a drag queen."

*

"I think that I'm perfect."

*

"All of my brothers and sisters are very talented. They all sang all right."

*

"My biggest extravagances are also investments. I have several houses in California, a house in Nashville, an office complex, and I bought the old home place in Tennessee. They are different places for me to write, but I can turn right around and sell them."

*

"I was always a junk food person, still am."

*

"I do have a lot of gays in my family now, but some will ncvcr come out."

*

"The only way I'd be caught without makeup is if my radio fell in the bathtub while I was taking a bath and electrocuted me and I was in between makeup at home. I hope my husband would slap a little lipstick on me before he took me to the morgue."

*

"If you like good ol' fashion Southern soul food then, yes, I am a good cook! My specialty is chicken dumplings and poke salad."

*

"I just don't feel like I have to explain myself."

*

"I do remember how it was to be poor. I do remember that in my early years, we had to grow and raise all of our food, even our animals. And I remember in my early life, we didn't even have electricity. So it was very, very hard times then."

*

"I have surrounded myself with very smart people."

*

"I've been around longer than most of my fans have
been alive."

*

"I think I became more productive through not
having children. I never really had the desire to
have them. My husband didn't want them either, so
it worked out well."

*

"Believe it or not, I was just given an honorary
doctorate degree from the University of Tennessee."

*

"I'm not trying to be fashionable. Never was!"

*

"I did not, thank the Lord, have to have a hysterectomy."

*

"Every single diet I ever fell off of was because of potatoes and gravy of some sort."

*

"I love being active."

*

"I've been very fortunate."

*

"I don't like to get involved in things that I am not familiar with. I'm kind of a hands-on type of person."

*

"I'm not offended by all the dumb blonde jokes
because I know I'm not dumb... and I also know that
I'm not blonde."

*

"I try not to go around looking like a hag."

HUMOROUS

"I was the first woman to burn my bra - it took the
fire department four days to put it out."

*

"I know some of the best Dolly Parton jokes. I made
'em up myself."

*

"I look just like the girls next door... if you happen
to live next door to an amusement park."

*

"I had to get rich so I could sing like I was poor again."

*

"People say I look so happy - and I say, 'That's the Botox.'"

*

"It costs a lot of money to look this cheap."

*

"Plastic surgeons are always making mountains out of molehills."

*

"The secret to a long marriage is to stay gone."

*

"Someone once asked me, 'How long does it take to do your hair.' I said, 'I don't know, I'm never there.'"

PHILOSOPHY

"Adjusting to the passage of time, I think, is a key to success and to life: just being able to roll with the punches."

*

"I feel that sin and evil are the negative part of you, and I think it's like a battery: you've got to have the negative and the positive in order to be a complete person."

*

"No one is ever successful at everything that they

do."

*

"I don't like to give advice. I like to give people information because everyone's life is different, and everyone's journey is different."

*

"You gotta keep trying to find your niche and trying to fit into whatever slot that's left for you or to make one of your own."

*

"Everybody has a purpose."

*

"I think everyone should be with who they love."

*

"Stop this attitude that older people ain't any good anymore! We're as good as we ever were - if we ever were any good."

*

"We cannot direct the wind, but we can adjust the sails."

*

"A lot of dreams can turn to nightmares... if you don't really work them."

*

"You'll never do a whole lot unless you're brave enough to try."

*

"You can be rich in spirit, kindness, love and all those things that you can't put a dollar sign on."

*

"The way I see it, if you want the rainbow, you gotta put up with the rain."

*

"Funny thing is that the poorer people are, the more generous they seem to be."

*

"If you don't like the road you're walking, start paving another one."

*

"I don't think you ever really know what all you're doing, so you have to act on faith."

*

"We're all just a bunch of sinners, but we do the best we can."

*

"Storms make trees take deeper roots."

*

"Find out who you are. And do it on purpose."

*

"Energy begets energy."

ALSO BY FRANK JOHNSON

INSIDE THE MIND OF CHUCK PALAHNIUK

THE WIT AND WISDOM OF JOSS WHEDON

THE VERY BEST OF MICHAEL MOORE

Made in United States
Troutdale, OR
12/28/2023